# PRAISE for RELENTLESS HOPE

*Relentless Hope* inspires followers of Christ to recommit to the local church as a worldwide movement of ordinary people doing the extraordinary work of mercy, justice, and peace. I highly recommend it.

—**Stephan Bauman**, Senior Vice President of Programs, World Relief

In *Relentless Hope*, you'll find a well-made case for local churches as communities of hope uniquely empowered to fulfill Jesus' call to disciple the nations, beginning with children, and doing so through global partnerships. *Relentless Hope* challenges each local church to become a center of missional transformation!

—**Bishop Hwa Yung**, The Methodist Church in Malaysia

In view of Dr. John Stott's concern that some churches show signs of "growth without depth," this book is a timely and passionate call for the Church to rediscover the depth of her commission. We are reminded to focus the mission of the Church on disciple-making, which moves beyond personal evangelism and church-planting and embraces the holistic transformation of community and culture.

Compassion International is being used by God as a "connector," to link the local Ecclesia and play an ongoing support role between them, with the goal of fulfilling the Great Commission.

—**Philemon Choi**, Breakthrough, Hon. General Secretary, Hong Kong

# Relentless HOPE

It is always exciting to read a book that focuses on what Christians have in common—their Savior and His mission, rather than what divides. *Relentless Hope* is such a book. With fresh language and compelling arguments, *Relentless Hope* articulates a comprehensive and intergenerational mission for the Ecclesia to be God's primary transformation agents in society. It is a call to throw off the shackles of defeatism and dependency and to use what God has placed in our hands to be His stewards of hope to a hurting and broken world.

*Relentless Hope*'s challenge is "Wake-up, Ecclesia! Christ has called you to challenge the very gates of hell. And they will not prevail against you!"

—**Darrow L. Miller**, author and cofounder of Disciple Nations Alliance

*Relentless Hope* unpacks God's plan for the restoration of all things through the Church. The Church accomplishes restoration by making disciples, with children as a priority focus.

—**Luis Bush**, International Facilitator, Transform World Connections

*Relentless Hope* offers a fresh hope to the 21st-century-global body of Christ. In a time of uncertainty, frustration, and agony for so many Christian institutions, especially in the global North, this book brings a new perspective on how to recover the biblical alignment of God's Ecclesia to transform the world. It is a MUST-read for kingdom global leaders.

—**Dr. David E. Ramirez**, Field Director to South America, Church of God World Missions

The Church is an unstoppable agent indeed. *Relentless Hope* helps the worldwide Christian community refocus on the place of the local church and challenges Christian leaders with a new vision of reaching children as the forces of transformation for the world.

—**Rev. Dr. Sang-Bok David Kim**, Chairman of the World Evangelical Alliance

It *is* a most compelling argument for a holistic approach to live out the hope of the gospel. This is a must-read for all who desire to see God's purposes fulfilled in His world!

—**Peter Chao**, Founder, Eagles Communications of Singapore

# Praise

When Jesus said, "I will build my church," He really did. This book gives us an insight into the Church's story of the Church's power—without arrogance.

—**Joel Edwards**, Executive Director of Micah Challenge International

If one shouldn't judge a room by its door, this book is just one. *Relentless Hope* is a small book with a decisive stroke of God's mission.

—**Wonsuk Ma**, PhD, Executive Director, David Yonggi Cho Research Tutor of Global Christianity, Oxford Centre for Mission Studies

Besides Jesus, my passion is for His bride, the Church. Why? Because she is the only human community expressly ordained to reveal God's cosmic purpose in and for our broken world. This little book does an excellent job of describing the "why" with a very strategic perspective on "how." If you want your church to fully participate in God's big agenda, this is a must-read.

—**Bob Moffitt**, author of *If Jesus Were Mayor*

The Ecclesia is the great hope of our ailing world. It is the divine entity empowered by agape love, equipped with heavenly authority, and placed in this world. Indeed, the Church has the power to change the world for good. Budijanto, Todd, and Yeadon make this truth about the Church come alive.

—**Aiah Foday-Khabenje**, General Secretary/CEO, Association of Evangelicals in Africa

In an age when many succumb to cynicism or despair, *Relentless Hope* kindles vitality and hope. Stirred by V.S. Azariah's vision, offered at the Edinburgh 1910 World Missionary Conference, of a united church powered by love, its authors issue a clarion call to rediscover the breathtaking spiritual force found in the New Testament church. Written with passion and compassion, *Relentless Hope* is a book which can change your life and transform the world.

—**Rev. Dr. Kenneth R. Ross**, Honorary Fellow of the Edinburgh University School of Divinity, former Secretary of the Church of Scotland World Mission Council

# RELENTLESS HOPE

## THE UNSTOPPABLE MOVEMENT OF DISCIPLE-MAKING COMMUNITIES

**Bambang Budijanto**
**Scott Todd**
**Mark Yeadon**

Copyright © 2010 by Compassion International
Published by Compassion International
Design and production by The Elevation Group
Cover photo: © iStockphoto.com/Ken Canning

All rights reserved. No part of this book may be reproduced without written permission, except for brief quotations in books and critical reviews. For information, write Compassion International, Colorado Springs, CO 80997.

Unless otherwise indicated, Scripture is taken from the *Holy Bible, New International Version*®. NIV®. Copyright © 1973, 1978, 1984 by International Bible Society. Used by permission of Zondervan Publishing House. All rights reserved.

Scripture quotations marked (NJKV) are taken from the *New King James Version*®. Copyright © 1979, 1980, 1982 by Thomas Nelson, Inc. Used by permission. All rights reserved.

Scripture marked MSG is taken from The Message by Eugene H. Peterson, copyright © 1993, 1994, 1995, 2000, 2001, 2002. Used by permission of NavPress Publishing Group. All rights reserved.

ISBN 978-0-9841169-5-9

Printed in Canada

10 9 8 7 6 5 4 3 2 1

# DEDICATION

To Liana, for your unwavering faith in Jesus and your unyielding confidence in me and our three children (Jemira, Melzar, and Arvad) in fulfilling His call for our lives.

To Bethany, for your joy and strength as we serve Him together.

To Teri, for the many years you have walked alongside of me, being a wonderful sounding board to an untold number of dreams, and pointing the path to Christlikeness through your example of love, patience, and kindness.

# CONTENTS

Preface
　xiii

About The Authors
　xvii

Introduction
　xxi

One: Stewards of Hope
　1

Two: The Ecclesia—God's Plan A
　15

Three: The One Thing—Disciple-Making
　37

Four: Children as Disciples
　61

Five: Global Connections, Local Relationships
　81

About Compassion International
　103

Notes
　105

# PREFACE

The premise of the book is that the Church is central to God's purpose for the world He created. Paul writes in his letter to the Ephesians that God's purpose is to bring all things in heaven and on earth under the Lordship of Christ (see Ephesians 1:9-10). And it is through Christ's body, the Church, the plan of God for His creation is made known to rulers and principalities in the heavenly realms. And so by God's Spirit, and through the death and resurrection of Christ, a new humanity is created in the Church as a sign of God's purpose for all humanity (see Ephesians 3:10-11).

The origin of the Church is in the person of the Triune God; the overflowing love in the three Persons of the Trinity calls forth the same kind of community as in the Trinity among human beings, and the Church is called

## Relentless HOPE

to reflect the outgoing love and unity of the Godhead. The essential mark of the Church is the public confession of Jesus as Lord in word and deed. The Church exists for confessing and demonstrating the Lordship of Christ in its life and mission.

The authors Budijanto, Todd, and Yeadon are senior leaders of Compassion International, a global ministry to children. They call us to recognize that the main drive for Christian mission must flow out of our understanding of the Church as God's primary plan and agent for His purpose for His creation. This gives those in mission both motivation and confidence as God's plan is unstoppable—the gates of hell will not prevail against it.

The book recovers the special place of the child in God's kingdom purposes. This is an often overlooked aspect of Jesus' teaching about the kingdom of God. A child not only mirrors the simplicity of the faith of the kingdom but also is a key agent of the transformation that the gospel of the kingdom brings.

# Preface

An unbelieving or curious world always judges the Christian faith by what the Church in its midst is and does. **This book enables us to recover a vision of the Church that is critical to our calling as Christians today.**

Rev'd Canon Dr. Vinay K. Samuel
Director, Oxford Centre for Religion and Public Life

# ABOUT THE AUTHORS

## Bambang Budijanto

Dr. Bambang Budijanto is the Vice President for the Asia Region at Compassion International.

He was the Founder and Executive Director of the Pesat Foundation in Indonesia from 1987 to 1997 and was the Founder and Director of the Institute for Community and Development Studies from 1997 to 1999. He currently serves on the Boards of the Pesat Foundation, the Institute for Community and Development Studies, the Oxford Centre for Mission Studies, and the Consortium for Graduate Programs in Christian Studies (CCS).

Dr. Budijanto also serves as the Director for Mission Commission of the Asia Evangelical Alliance and as a member of the Editorial Board for Transformation Journal. He received his Ph.D. from the Oxford Centre for Mission Studies and the University of Wales.

# Relentless HOPE

## Scott Todd

Dr. Scott Todd is the Senior Ministry Advisor in the President's Office at Compassion International. During his tenure at Compassion he has served as Director of the AIDS Initiative, Child Survival Program, and Complementary Interventions—a set of programs ranging from disaster response to Bible distribution. Dr. Todd is Chairman of the Board of Directors for Association of Relief and Development Organizations (AERDO) and serves on the Board of Micah Challenge USA. He oversees Compassion's global advocacy efforts and represents Compassion in networks focused on missions, development and children.

A passionate follower of Jesus Christ, Dr. Todd left academic research in 2003 to join Compassion International. He believes that this generation of Christians can and, by God's grace, will end extreme global poverty.

## About The Authors

### Mark Yeadon

Soon after his employment with Compassion International began in 1984, Mark Yeadon accepted a position in their South America Area Office and moved his family to Quito, Ecuador. He served in Ecuador for three years as Compassion's Associate Director of Operations and for four years as their Area Director for South America.

In 1993, Mark accepted the position of Program Director at Compassion's Global Ministry Center and moved his family to Colorado Springs where they now reside. In his current position as Sr. Vice President of International Program, he is responsible for providing the leadership of Compassion's program development and management worldwide.

# INTRODUCTION

A century ago, a dignified, soft-spoken church leader from India stood before a conference of world church leaders in Edinburgh, Scotland. He had just a few minutes to deliver what God had put on his heart, and it would not be easy.

Nonetheless, V. S. Azariah commented openly on the uncomfortable relationship between Christians in India and European missionaries. "Friendship is more than condescending love….Too often you promise us thrones in heaven, but will not offer us chairs in your drawing rooms."[1]

Azariah elaborated on the nature of the relationship between indigenous Christians and missionaries, but soon moved to the real point of his remarks.

# Relentless HOPE

> The exceeding riches of the glory of Christ can be fully realised not by the Englishman, the American, and the Continental alone, nor by the Japanese, the Chinese, and the Indians by themselves—but by all working together, worshipping together, and learning together the Perfect Image of our Lord and Christ.[2]

Working, worshipping, and learning together to better conform to Christ is both a command and an ideal for Christians. But keeping the Church moving in the same direction to further her mission has been at least as challenging as keeping the children of Israel moving through the wilderness to reach the Promised Land. It took years, for example, for the Church to agree that the call to make disciples should reach beyond the Jewish community. Over time, the Church would become like an arm of the government in some places and forced underground in others. As the Church spread geographically, she sometimes reflected the dominant culture more than she reflected the life and teachings of Jesus.

## Introduction

But there were also times when the Church was light and life in a context of great darkness. The Church profoundly impacted cultures as Christianity spread—promoting equality, justice, literacy, and compassion. Yet the expansion of Christianity also brought people of very diverse cultures into the Church, and Christians from different cultures sometimes focused on their differences rather than their common mission. Thus Azariah's remarks at the 1910 World Missionary Conference at Edinburgh—calling the Church to unite around her mission instead of divide over cultural biases.

> **God does not lead a movement of abstract ideas; He leads a movement of people.**

The 20th century was marked by a shift in the focus of Christian activity from the global North to the global South[3]—a dynamic anticipated by leaders of both hemispheres who were present at the Edinburgh conference in 1910. These changing global dynamics are having a profound impact on Christianity.[4] Influential voices from the global South are shaping theology, presenting new leadership, changing the dynamics of mission, and offering new perspective on the Church. Yet all of these global changes and new ideas must translate into application and find their meaning within local churches to become locally relevant. God does not lead a movement of abstract ideas; He leads a movement of people. And those people live and worship together as local expressions of the body of Christ within communities.

Why does God insist on working with communities of believers? The Lord Jesus Christ commissioned these dynamic communities to go to all peoples and make disciples. They would have to deliver the gospel, breaking down cultural barriers to fulfill this epic calling. One entity, at God's direction and blessing, would overcome the very gates of hell to change the course of both life and eternity. They would be unstoppable.

These communities of believers sometimes falter. They are not perfect. They make mistakes. They make excuses. Yet God commissioned and empowered these communities to complete the Great Commission. They are God's Plan A, and there is no Plan B.

# Introduction

The pages that follow will outline a simple response to this reality through five short essays.

- First, we make the case for churches being stewards of relentless hope.

- Second, we examine God's call on the Church to embody both His person and His work.

- Third, we explore the strategy for disciple-making in the context of community.

- Fourth, we consider the importance of lifelong disciple-making and the impact of intentional spiritual development for children.

- Finally, we discuss the interaction between global connections and local relationships in optimizing the advance of God's kingdom. This topic is particularly important as local fellowships in the North and South learn to help each other toward that goal.

In no way is this book positioned to become "the final word" on the Church and her mission. Instead, we hope it galvanizes action for which God and our neighbors have waited far too long.

In our work with Compassion International, we have the privilege of partnering with over 5,000 churches in the global South. These churches represent the full spectrum of Protestant Christianity. We also have the privilege of partnering with hundreds of thousands of Christians and churches across North America, Europe, Australia, New Zealand, and South Korea. With over 57 years of working with churches, we have a unique vantage point to observe God's movement among His people. We have seen the world-changing transformation that comes when God's people, as the local dynamic community—the Ecclesia—respond to the call to make disciples of all nations.

This is a small book about a big idea—and the big idea isn't ours. Together, Christians have the opportunity to turn history and transform this world. To do so we, as Christ-followers, must commit to the unique role of the Ecclesia. We must wholeheartedly support the Ecclesia's task of disciple-making. We must remember it

## Introduction

will take all of us—Northern and Southern Christians—working together to fulfill God's mandate.

The Ecclesia is God's ordained Plan A to transform the world. This is not an impossible and abstract task. Instead, it is a calling to change the core of the very harsh realities that our families, neighbors, and local and global communities face every day. From the rise of the nondenominational church in the West to house churches in China, we are witnessing the Ecclesia take on new life as it rediscovers its role in kingdom work. In the light of this changing kingdom landscape, vast parachurch and denominational structures must prayerfully reexamine their roles as they relate to the Ecclesia. God is moving His people away from institutions and toward holistic communities of Christian faith representative of the Acts 2 church. We write to affirm this movement, to celebrate the work of God among His people, and to encourage church leaders of the Southern as well as Northern churches in their work.

For clarity's sake, let us briefly explain what we mean when we use "ecclesia." While "ecclesia" was a Greek word commonly used prior to and during Jesus' time, Jesus did not confine His idea of ecclesia to the

Greco-Roman usage, which referred to sociopolitical gatherings. Jesus gave a fresh connotation to the word, later developed by Luke and Paul. Instead of an event or gathering, He presented the Ecclesia as primarily a dynamic kingdom community, an unstoppable spiritual force on earth, and an eschatological agent of transformation.[5] So when we use the word, we think more of the dynamism that advances God's kingdom and less of a static institution. We also use "ecclesia" almost exclusively in reference to a local body of believers, because of the primacy given to the local Christian community in the New Testament.

May God grant the Ecclesia courage and grace to be His agent of change for this generation.

**Bambang Budijanto**
**Scott Todd**
**Mark Yeadon**

*Colorado Springs, CO*
*March 2010*

# ONE
# STEWARDS OF
# HOPE

## Relentless HOPE

Human history is, in part, a story of pain and brokenness. God created us in a state of perfection. Yet, by our own actions, we bring pain into that perfection. That pain manifests in everything from our damaged marriages to our national wars; from personal depression to global poverty.

The whole of human suffering is linked to our sins—our greed, insecurities, jealousies, selfishness, ambition, lust, and worship of anything but the one true God. We hope in the wrong things: military might, our own wisdom, political systems, or wealth, for example. As those things in which we have misplaced hope fail, we lose our capacity to hope.

Broken and insecure people build systems of self-preservation that oppress and dehumanize others. Child soldiers suffer much the same way as did children in Nazi concentration camps. They are deprived of any sense of the future. They lose hope for what could be.

Life without hope can feel suffocating. People feel the crush of another week without enough work and wonder where the next meal is coming from. A father hears the doctor pronounce a diagnosis on his child, knowing he has neither the knowledge nor money to save his child's life. A single mother searches the eyes of her teenage daughter, knowing the girl has given up on trying to remain a virgin.

Yet hope drives one's outlook for the future. A recent Gallup research shows hope is a better indicator for student success in college than secondary school performance (high school grades). There are also correlations between hope and community involvement, employment, and problem solving. The survey showed, however, that only half of the students surveyed felt hopeful. The other half was characterized by the study as "stuck or discouraged."[1] Life without hope can leave one feeling that way.

> **Indeed, we can think of the Ecclesia, the Church, as stewards of God's relentless hope for a waiting, despairing world.**

Hope is oxygen. It circulates and sustains the body. Without it we collapse. Perhaps that's why Paul encouraged the early Christians to nurture hope through endurance and the encouragement of the Scriptures.[2] In the same way, the Hebrew Christians were charged to be agents of hope to others through their acts of service. As they gave others hope, their own hope would be built up.[3]

Indeed, we can think of the Ecclesia, the Church, as stewards of God's relentless hope for a waiting, despairing world.

## Jesus Launches the Movement of Hope Stewards

Jesus' own teaching on the judgment set the standard for His followers then as today. Matthew 25:34-40 is clear:

> Then the King will say to those on his right, "Come, you who are blessed by my Father; take your inheritance, the kingdom prepared for you since the creation of the world. For I was hungry and you gave me something to eat, I was thirsty and

you gave me something to drink, I was a stranger and you invited me in, I needed clothes and you clothed me, I was sick and you looked after me, I was in prison and you came to visit me."

Then the righteous will answer him, "Lord, when did we see you hungry and feed you, or thirsty and give you something to drink? When did we see you a stranger and invite you in, or needing clothes and clothe you? When did we see you sick or in prison and go to visit you?"

The King will reply, "I tell you the truth, whatever you did for one of the least of these brothers of mine, you did for me."

The Early Church actually took these words seriously. They embraced their role as ecclesia with a clear vision to help those in need. As an epidemic swept through his land, the early church leader Eusebius wrote,

## Relentless HOPE

> But after both we and they had enjoyed a very brief season of rest this pestilence assailed us; to them more dreadful than any dread, and more intolerable than any other calamity; and, as one of their own writers has said, the only thing which prevails over all hope. But to us this was not so…. The most of our brethren were unsparing in their exceeding love and brotherly kindness. They held fast to each other and visited the sick fearlessly, and ministered to them continually, serving them in Christ. And they died with them most joyfully, taking the affliction of others, and drawing the sickness from their neighbors to themselves and willingly receiving their pains. And many who cared for the sick and gave strength to others died themselves having transferred to themselves their death.[4]

Eusebius described a dread that "prevails over all hope." Yet it did not prevail over the hope of Christ. It did not drive Jesus' disciples into hiding or fear. They continued ministering fearlessly. They were stewards of hope to those whose hope was lost.

Yet at other times, it was also necessary for church leaders to remind Christians to put their faith into action. Only then could they provide hope for others and build their own hope in Christ.

The Jerusalem church leader James reminded 1st-century Christians to care for their brothers in need, even defining "pure religion" as living a moral life that includes care for widows and orphans.[5] In fact, Christians identified so much with the poor, in some cities of the Roman Empire, they were considered second-class citizens economically. (In many cases, that was true.)

Spurred by the possibilities of being stewards of hope, Christians have often ministered where few others will go. Christians were among the first to minister to the victims of the Black Death in medieval Europe. In so doing, they brought hope to those overwhelmed by the ravages of disease and death. They made literacy a priority for the common people, so all could read the Bible. As a result, generations were equipped with the ability to read and advance both their knowledge base and economic well-being. They championed the case for abolition when slavery was thought to be an economic necessity in the United Kingdom and the United States. This reversed a worldview that counted some people as mere property.

The legacy of transforming culture through the influence of the gospel is uniquely tied to the making of disciples. Seasoned disciples flattened economic discrimination in the 1st-century ecclesia in Jerusalem, fought for the Universal Declaration of Human Rights in the 20th century, and stood strong to replace child labor with child education from the 18th century forward. They were simply putting their faith in action—stewarding hope.

Today, the stewarding of hope through the Ecclesia takes shape in a variety of practical ministries. Christians organize and staff literacy programs for at-risk children and adults around the world. Churches become centers for distributing food and medical assistance during disasters such as the Indonesian tsunami of 2004 and the Haiti earthquake of 2010. Churches host training in job skills. They run soup kitchens. Across Africa they distribute insecticide-treated mosquito nets to protect people from malaria. And through it all, the Ecclesia communicates the love and truth of the gospel as best it can.

One ecclesia just outside of Jakarta embraces families whose fathers are imprisoned. The ministry team there sees to it that these families have adequate nutrition. They teach job skills to older children and mothers. They provide a safe haven for the children of these families. They provide a place where the children and spouses of prisoners can talk about the challenges they face. They offer the gospel to those who will listen.

Then there is the ecclesia in Denver, with a team of volunteers who are on call to clean up after someone commits suicide. It is a service that, before the team's inception, was left to the family or friends of a suicide victim. The impact of cleaning up after a loved one took his own life is brutal. The team's ministry was received quickly and gratefully by the community services— legal, social, and spiritual alike—traditionally involved in such cases.

These ministries were birthed in prayer and out of God giving someone a vision for another category of "the least of these." Sometimes the families these teams serve show up for a church service. Sometimes they don't. Yet the very presence of these ministries of the local ecclesia at a time of great need speaks hope to those who truly need it.

## The Common Thread and the Passion for the Possible

The common thread running through all those who take on the role of being a steward of hope is this: *at some point, they each believe they are God's unstoppable Plan A for their given situation—and there is no Plan B.*

These are people whose very being resonates with Jesus' pronouncement regarding the Church founded by Him. Simply put, "I will build my church; and the gates of hell will not prevail against it" (Matthew 16:18, KJV). They will take action that matters. They will be God's agents to shatter darkness with the hope of Jesus Christ. They look at what others say are "impossible" situations and turn those situations upside down.

Soren Kierkegaard once characterized a living and vibrant faith as one that had a "passion of the possible."[6] Just as important, Kierkegaard came to realize that Jesus Christ has made all things possible (see Mark 10:27). Things that were once unimaginable come into clarity. Possibilities for world-changing service expand exponentially. One may begin believing that he cannot change anything. But becoming a disciple changes the person. Disciples end up embracing the fact that they are not only called but are actually equipped to advance God's kingdom.

> **Those painful things that should be changed can be changed; from ending global poverty to healing a marriage.**

Because God has shown us the impossible in raising Christ from the dead, all things have been made possible. That means our opportunities to be stewards of hope are unlimited. Without boundaries. Those painful things that *should* be changed *can* be changed; from ending global poverty to healing a marriage.

## Relentless HOPE

It is even possible to become part of God's transforming power. God's desire for our complete, holistic transformation is nowhere more clear and powerful than the greatest commandment: "'Love the Lord your God with all your heart and with all your soul and with all your mind and with all your strength.' The second is this: 'Love your neighbor as yourself'" (Mark 12:30-31). The love of God is to emanate from every aspect of our being—body, mind, emotions, and social relationships. Loving God is more than just a mental exercise. It is an act of our whole being. In the same way, our love for others is expressed from our whole being. God wants to engage our whole person in loving and serving Him. This makes the possibilities for serving others almost endless.

## The Context for Stewarding Hope

As we will see in the essays that follow, as the Church makes authentic disciples, it develops a people who not only strengthen the Church but also advance the reconciling work of God in our world.

The implications of this mission for our hurting world are nothing less than revolutionary. While church leadership creates an environment and facilitates growth for every individual member in the context of community, it is their service to others that will strengthen the body of Christ and create transformation and growth in their lives. Without service, there is no spiritual growth.

> From whom the whole body, joined and knit together by what every joint supplies, according to the effective working by which every part does its share, causes growth of the body for the edifying of itself in love. (Ephesians 4:16, NJKV)

The dynamic community of the Ecclesia of Jesus Christ powerfully operates in advancing the kingdom of God every single day, seven days a week, as we serve and grow to be more like Christ. Unfortunately, this continuous transformation we see in the historic Church has often been reduced into a single event on Sunday. In so doing, we strip it of the new meaning Jesus invested in the term when He designated it for His kingdom community. It returns it to its old secular usage as merely an event or a gathering.

In stark contrast, C. S. Lewis reminds us, "The Church exists for nothing else but to draw men into Christ, to make them little Christs. If they are not doing that, all the cathedrals, clergy, missions, sermons, even the Bible itself, are simply a waste of time."[7]

Christ's plan for the future of this broken world is to restore His kingdom. Jesus declared His plan when He gave His disciples the Great Commission. The task is so huge. But Christ's strategy is very simple and focused: make disciples. Why? Disciples are stewards of hope. Stewards of hope deliver God's ongoing, holistic, and eternal plan for redemption and reconciliation.

And this task is given to the Church, the power-filled Ecclesia. The work of restoring and advancing the kingdom of God is a job *only* the Ecclesia of Jesus Christ can do. There is no Plan B. The Ecclesia is God's chosen mechanism to steward—and release—the unique and relentless hope present in Jesus Christ.

# TWO
## THE ECCLESIA—
# God's Plan A

## Relentless HOPE

Jesus had completed His work on earth. Between the time of His resurrection and ascension, He continued to lay the foundation for the Ecclesia before hundreds who followed Him.[1] His commandment to make disciples in all the world was clear.[2] The goal was the very restoration of the kingdom of God through making disciples. The Ecclesia, as a kingdom community, would be the primary agent and witness to fulfill the task as empowered by the Holy Spirit.[3]

> **Jesus set forth one and only one strategy for the rescue of our world from its troubled course.**

Jesus set forth one and only one strategy for the rescue of our world from its troubled course. Had there been any other, Jesus surely would have taught about it in His ministry on earth, and especially in the 40 days between His resurrection and ascension. But the only entity of transformation in which Jesus invested His time and teaching was this Ecclesia.

In the Ecclesia, Jesus began and sustains a movement of people, a dynamic community of ambassadors empowered by His very Spirit to accomplish His mission of redemption. This community is not just an inwardly focused place of belonging. It is salt. It is light. It is to transform the world.

## The Ecclesia: Unstoppable Force

The Ecclesia is the primary agent God chooses, establishes, and nurtures to accomplish His purpose in establishing His kingdom on earth. She is the only agency established by Jesus Christ, as seen in Matthew 16:18-19:

> And I tell you that you are Peter, and on this rock I will build my church, and the gates of Hades will not overcome it. I will give you the keys of the kingdom of heaven; whatever you bind on earth will be bound in heaven, and whatever you loose on earth will be loosed in heaven.

Jesus was the founder, the architect, and the One who, by the power of the Holy Spirit, constructed and established the Ecclesia *par excellence* in Acts 2. Through His Holy Spirit, Jesus is also the one who continues to build, edify, and embolden His Ecclesia everywhere and throughout church history.

The Ecclesia was meant to be a dynamic, progressive, transforming community for the advancement of the kingdom of God, both in individual lives as well as in community. The advancement of life (see John 10:10) and the kingdom of God implies the weakening and shrinkage of the kingdom of death and darkness. Thus the Ecclesia, by her very nature, poses a serious threat to Hades (death) and the kingdom of hell (Sheol).

Apparently, the Ecclesia is the *only* plan Jesus has to redeem His creation. There is no mention of any other entity anywhere in the New Testament. The Church is the body of which Christ is the Head.[4] He did not establish any other agency or introduce any Plan B to accomplish His mission. He did not establish a new government—although that is what people expected of their Messiah. Rather, by the power of Jesus' resurrection and the power of the Holy Spirit, He established the Ecclesia, the unstoppable force to advance His kingdom. Even the gates of hell would not be able to stop her, let alone overcome this dynamic kingdom community.

Jesus also indicated that the Ecclesia would possess the keys of the kingdom, which would grant an unlimited access to the throne of God. With this privilege, the Ecclesia would operate in the "authority" and power of God. With the magnitude of the mission and the threat she posed to the kingdom of hell, the Ecclesia could not afford to operate within the human realm relying only on human strength. The Ecclesia in Acts 2 set the standard for what it means to operate in the power of God.[5]

Think of it: *why would Jesus give so much power to the Church if He didn't intend for her to achieve His goals?* Through disciple-making, the Ecclesia is called to bring people far from Christ close to Christ—and then into Christlikeness.

## The Ecclesia in Acts 2: Advancing, Not Static

The Ecclesia is built for action. She is a force established to face extreme challenges and to prevail against extreme opposition. She was founded upon the "rock," a firm, unmovable foundation, and endowed with power from on high to ensure that she would prevail against the gates of Hades. And after the Ecclesia was inaugurated in Jerusalem in Acts 2, she spread out and, less than 200 years later, had transformed the known world.

Consider the first-generation ecclesia. The Acts 2 church is the materialization, expression, and demonstration of the Ecclesia as designed by Jesus. The power and working of the Holy Spirit was evident in their midst. Just consider what happened with this small group of people in a short period of time:

- The power of the Holy Spirit filled the community with courage. The Ecclesia became an uncompromisingly courageous community, speaking boldly, astonishing their listeners, and even shaking the walls.[6]

## The Ecclesia – God's Plan A

- They had a high sense of calling and determination, not faltering when flogged, but rejoicing in suffering.[7]

- They showed genuine love and deep care for each other, committing themselves to daily fellowship.[8]

- They practiced extreme generosity; their love informed their actions, and there were no needy people among them.[9]

- The heart and mind of the believers were united.[10]

- Jesus confirmed their testimony with great signs and wonders. People looked at the Ecclesia with great respect and awe.[11]

- From day one, the Ecclesia became a dynamically growing, disciple-making community.[12]

This small community shook up their world and altered the course of history. The Acts 2 church offers a design for us. Consider these descriptions. Do they describe your own local church today? Even more, how can we replicate the Acts 2 design today?

## Relentless HOPE

To answer that question, we need to revisit our understanding of the Church.

> **This is no meeting. This is a force that will change the world.**

# What Is the Ecclesia?

Let's face it: few of us would say that our own church looks just like the Acts 2 church. The Acts 2 church challenges our experience with church—and challenges us to take a serious look at the scriptural concept of ecclesia. A biblical understanding of the Church is key to understanding our part in the Great Commission.

The Greek word *ecclesia*, translated in the New Testament as *church*, was common prior to and during Jesus' time. It referred to a summons for the army to assemble. Later, *ecclesia* was used to denote a popular or general assembly for a civic purpose or a sociopolitical gathering in Athena. Overall, it conveyed the meaning of "a gathering of people" or "an event where people gathered together in one place for sociopolitical purposes."

Yet Jesus did not confine His idea of ecclesia to the secular usage. Jesus gave a *new* connotation to the word. Instead of a mere event or gathering, Jesus presented the Ecclesia as an unstoppable force on earth and an agent of transformation of the eternal fate of man. Again, in Matthew 16:18: "And I tell you that you are Peter, and on this rock I will build my church, and the gates of Hades will not overcome it," Jesus' use of the word *ecclesia* is clear: This is no meeting. This is a force that will change the world.

There are three different ways *ecclesia* is used in the New Testament. One usage of *ecclesia* refers to *gatherings of the people of God*.[13] Most of the occurrences of *ecclesia* in the oldest Greek translation of the New Testament (Septuagint) are in this category; similar to the way the word was used in the secular world at that time.

The second usage is as an allegory, using the human body as an illustration of the Church and describing

## Relentless HOPE

Jesus Christ as the Head.[14] In this usage, Jesus Christ as the Head guides and directs the body. Another allegorical use likens the relationship between the Lord Jesus and the Ecclesia to the relationship between a husband and wife.[15] Jesus Christ as the Husband protects and loves the Ecclesia, and the Ecclesia respects and is faithful to serve her Lord. So the Ecclesia isn't just a meeting—she is represented as *a living body guided by Christ in an intimate relationship*.

The third major use of *ecclesia* in the New Testament refers to the actual community of the believers, a congregation of God's people within a geographical location. The Ecclesia is definable by geographical limits.[16] In the book of Acts, 19 of the 23 instances of *ecclesia* refer to local church congregations. *Ecclesia* is also used throughout Paul's letters and in the writing of James and the apostle John, almost exclusively referring to a local community of believers. So, the Ecclesia isn't just an event or an abstract concept, but *a local community of people in relationship with one another*.

These uses of *ecclesia* reveal the attitude of the Acts 2 church and why it was so different from anything seen before on this earth: They weren't just a meeting.

They were called out and called together to transform their world. They were a community, a body, locally committed to one another. They were headed, led, and loved by the Lord Jesus Christ. And they were an unstoppable spiritual force. They were defined as family as Jesus defined family: those who were doing the will of the Father.[17]

## The Turning Point for the Ecclesia

While Luke uses the word *ecclesia* 23 times in the book of Acts, he does not use the term at all in his gospel. This suggests that he and the other authors of the gospels perhaps consciously avoided using the word *ecclesia* for any group of disciples or believers during the period of Jesus' earthly activity. The turning point that transformed Jesus' followers into the Ecclesia of Jesus Christ was the outpouring of the Holy Spirit in Acts 2.

The Day of Pentecost is the birthday of the Ecclesia. As recorded in Acts 1:8, Jesus predicted when the Ecclesia would be born, characterizing the new community with divine power:

## Relentless HOPE

> But you will receive power when the Holy Spirit comes on you; and you will be my witnesses in Jerusalem, and in all Judea and Samaria, and to the ends of the earth.

What turned this new community from just a gathering into the dynamic unstoppable community of Ecclesia? It was the power of the Holy Spirit, which was now operating in and through the lives of every member of the Ecclesia. This same group of people who had been fearful and weak[18] suddenly emerged into a courageous and powerful community—the Ecclesia. And this is the same ecclesia we see turning the world upside down, transforming their community, and making disciples daily.

## Ecclesia: Agent of the Kingdom

The Church is the agent of the kingdom of God. Her mission is to establish the reign of God in every aspect of individual life and society throughout the ages. This is the great hope of the world—not our national governments, not business, not universities, not good diets, not the G8, G20, or any other human establishment. Through the Ecclesia, the reign of God is most vividly demonstrated in the lives of her members, both at the individual and the social level. The Ecclesia will live up to this call as her members continue to be transformed into the likeness of Christ.

The leadership and structure in the Early Church were meant to facilitate this continuous transformation of each member into a mature believer in the likeness of Christ. In Ephesians 4:11-13, the apostle Paul remarks,

> [God] gave some to be apostles, some to be prophets, some to be evangelists, and some to be pastors and teachers, to prepare God's people for works of service, so that the body of Christ may be built up until we all reach unity in the faith and in the knowledge of the Son of God and become mature, attaining to the whole measure of the fullness of Christ.

The equipping and growth of individuals, the disciple-making process, is to take place in the context of the Ecclesia and is to result in "works of service." This is intrinsic to "attaining to the whole measure of the fullness of Christ." The path of becoming like Christ is one we walk *in community*, and it is two-way—we receive in order to give, and in giving, we receive and grow. Internal growth is only made complete in outward expression of Spirit-led obedience, and Spirit-led obedience generates true internal growth.

While church leadership creates an environment and facilitates growth for every individual member in the context of community, it is their service to others that will strengthen the body of Christ and create transformation and growth in their lives. Without service, there is no spiritual growth. As Paul encouraged the Early Church in Ephesus in Ephesians 4:16,

> From whom the whole body, joined and knit together by what every joint supplies, according to the effective working by which every part does its share, causes growth of the body for the edifying of itself in love. (NKJV)

## The Ecclesia – God's Plan A

Consider the service of the Good Shepherd Baptist Church to the community of Leon Brindis, a remote village of roughly 300 families in the Mexican state of Chiapas. Their ministry to children made them keenly aware of health issues facing the village. The community does not have any kind of sanitary services. People normally dig their own latrines and either carry water from the community well or buy the water in small containers. Since the people live in the wilderness, mosquitoes and malaria are also a big health concern. In response, the Good Shepherd Baptist Church has organized community cleaning campaigns, trash can placement, and trash collection for the village. Thanks to the church's community advocacy efforts, the local government now coordinates regular fumigations to kill mosquitoes and to prevent malaria outbreaks in the area. With these simple steps, the community has improved not only appearance but also decreased the risk of malaria.

Churches sometimes think that doing good work in community is separate from disciple-making. But doing good work in community is itself disciple-making. Jesus healed people from their physical diseases. He cared for people physically, and in doing so, He drew people into a relationship with their Savior. When the church expresses God's love through practical action, such as helping protect a community from malaria, it has the same effect. Love expressed in practical terms is real, not theory. People become curious about that love and are drawn into a relationship with their Savior. That is disciple-making. Of course, it does not stand alone. Good works are not sufficient to make disciples, but they are indispensable. Paul wrote to the Galatian Ecclesia, "The only thing that counts is faith expressing itself in love."[19] In Chiapas, faith is expressing itself in practical terms like malaria prevention work and cleaning up trash.

The dynamic community of Jesus Christ powerfully operates in advancing the kingdom of God every single day, seven days a week, as we serve and grow to be more like Christ. The Ecclesia is not reduced to a single event on Sunday. She is God's agent to transform society when "church" isn't just a once-a-week event, but is a growing body: every part doing its share, participating in acts of service, and maturing to attain the full measure of Christ.

# A Dynamic Disciple-Making Kingdom Community

The Ecclesia of Jesus Christ is built to let God's power and purpose flow through her to transform and redeem His creation. For many, that requires looking at "church" in a new way. We have found five common characteristics that describe strong ecclesia around the world. These cannot be counted as the only definitive characteristics, but are worth considering.

**First, their primary emphasis in faith community is on the local, not the universal, body of believers.** Once a person becomes a Christian, he or she becomes a member of the universal body of Christ. Christ unites them with every other Christian in spirit. But this universal membership in the body of Christ is given concrete expression in the form of the local church. Ephesians 3:6 calls it a mystery that Gentiles and Jews are now members of one body. And that was only the start. The reconciliatory work of Christ goes much further, as Galatians 3:28 demonstrates; free men and slaves, men and women, rich and poor, all become part of this body as the visible sign of the reconciling power of Jesus Christ. But the people of God must have a visible, local expression—a community of people that is empowered through the indwelling of the Holy Spirit to do what Jesus commanded them to do, make disciples.

**Second, their practice of faith is a lifestyle, not a weekly event.** Protestant ecclesiology has placed much emphasis on the preaching of the Word and the proper administration of the sacraments.[20] Over time this has led to a reduced understanding of church as merely the place we go once a week to receive biblical exposition, right doctrine, and the sacraments. While there is no question that the weekly coming together as a community is important for worship and instruction ("there is a need for structures that facilitate a balanced, three-dimensional life through worship, community and mission"[21]), a true biblical understanding of the church does not support such reductionism. The Ecclesia share their lives 24/7 and view living as a disciple-making community a lifestyle rather than an event.

**Third, healthy ecclesia perceive the church more as an organism and less as an organization.** Jim Engel and Bill Dyrness wrote, "The institutionalized form of the church has distorted its own nature of the living body of Christ in the world... In reality... the church is more like a living and responsive *organism* than an *organization*."[22]

While every church has to find her most appropriate form of structure and governance, Jesus rejected hierarchical views for His followers and put the main emphasis on the organic community sharing and serving in humility for the benefit of all.[23]

**Fourth, the impetus of strong ecclesia is to build community, not an institution.** All Christian organizations (seminaries, denominations, faith-based NGOs, mission boards, publishing houses, etc.) are only supportive structures created to serve the local church in her life and mission. As Snyder points out, "One of the greatest needs of the institutional church today is for a clear and sharp distinction between the church as biblically presented and the varied, subsidiary, ecclesiastical institutions, including denominational structures, that we so frequently confuse with the church."[24]

It is, of course, understandable that the church has an institutional side to it as a social reality with identifiable features. But the essence of the church is not found in being an institution, although it has institutional forms and appearances. This would be confusing the wine and the wineskin.

**Fifth, active ecclesia identify more strongly with living stones than buildings.**

The Greek word *kyriake* with its original meaning "of the Lord" became in early church history synonymous with the "Lord's Day" and later with the "church building." This usage paved the way for the sad misunderstanding of the church as being simply a building where you go. Again, church buildings are not a problem in and of themselves. It is the identification of the Ecclesia as a building that is problematic. The biblical emphasis is clear: we are a living temple and living stones that build a spiritual house.[25] The primary focus must be on *the community of God's people* and not the buildings they occupy.

# There Is No Plan B

Again, the Ecclesia is God's Plan A for transforming

the world. Jesus put no other option in place. If God's will is to be enacted in our generation, it is up to the Ecclesia.

It is up to us because families, governments, and other social structures—as important as they are—cannot take on the role and responsibilities of the Ecclesia. Certainly we cannot devalue what other entities have to offer. But none of them can take the strategic place of the Ecclesia in transformation through disciple-making.

Is the Ecclesia willing to abandon the ideas, perceptions, and activity that impede the power and purposes of God from flowing freely through her? Is she willing to make the Ecclesia a 24/7 commitment? Will the disciples of the Ecclesia seek out ways to transform people and communities to advance God's agenda?

John Westerhoff III notes,

> The church is a human association of a particular kind. It is not a 'natural' group like a biological family; it is not a group based solely on common interests

like a club; it is not a provider of goods and services like a corporation; it is not a voluntary association to meet and protect the interests of its members like the American Medical Association. The church is the Ecclesia of God, a gathering of people called out to be something and to do something together on behalf of everyone: a covenant community whose purpose is to serve others.[26]

Can the Ecclesia stop poverty, oppression, and alter the very course of history? According to Jesus, the Ecclesia is unstoppable. He built the Ecclesia for nothing less—and there is no Plan B.

# THREE
# THE ONE THING—
# Disciple-Making

## Relentless HOPE

Guided by the Holy Spirit, disciple-making is a dynamic journey of holistic personal growth in becoming like Jesus. It happens

- in, with, and through the kingdom community (ecclesia);
- within the context, and for the purpose, of advancing God's reign (the Lordship of Christ);
- in individual life as well as in the broader community setting.

**Evangelism is a crucial part of disciple-making—but it is not the whole of disciple-making.**

*Being a disciple is*, of course, the result of disciple-making. It also happens in the context of the Ecclesia and under the Lordship of Christ—and in individual as well as community life.

# The One Thing — Disciple-Making

Being a disciple is interdependent with making disciples. Ultimately, God makes disciples and we participate with Him in that work. The Holy Spirit calls, convicts, guides, and empowers the disciple along the journey. Much of the Holy Spirit's work is done through other disciples living in obedience—demonstrating the Lordship of Christ in their own lives. So our being a disciple is a major vehicle through which God makes disciples of others.

It takes disciples to make disciples. The Ecclesia seeks to fulfill the only agenda Jesus gave to it: the Great Commission. Evangelism is a crucial part of disciple-making—but it is not the whole of disciple-making. Make no mistake, this agenda is not about learning a series of three, five, or seven principles on a weekend retreat and being able to recite them afterward. It is about a revolution of our loyalties, a recalibration to the leading of the Holy Spirit, which breathes life into our character, our actions, and our relationships. It is comprehensive life-change that continually moves toward Christ and draws others toward Christ.

Disciple-making is the transformation strategy of God's kingdom. As stated in the previous essay, "the reign of God is most vividly demonstrated in the lives of her members, both at the individual and the social level. The Ecclesia will live up to this call as her members continue to be transformed into the likeness of Christ."

So, where are we, as the Ecclesia, in the process of living up to our call?

# The Great Commission and Today's Church

Many pastors and Christian leaders have recognized the abundance of "nondisciple Christians." They describe churches with a heavy presence of these consumer Christians and their associated expectations, which are hindering the church from even seeing disciple-making as their role. Many churches have relegated the task of disciple-making to parachurch organizations.

In their book *Jesus Wants to Save Christians*, Rob Bell and Don Golden remind us that the church is not a center for religious goods and services. Her business is not to meet the market demands of a target demographic.[1]

## The One Thing — Disciple-Making

But what is the state of today's ecclesia? Are we making disciples or meeting a consumer niche? How do our leaders understand disciple-making? How engaged in disciple-making are the churches of the world?

Compassion International recently surveyed some 900 evangelical pastors of different denominational affiliations from 25 countries in the global South (Asia, Africa, and Latin America). Approximately 20 percent of these pastors defined disciple-making as confession of Jesus as personal Savior. Another 20 percent defined it as Bible study classes, groups, or meetings. Close to 60 percent saw disciple-making as a process of growth in becoming like Jesus Christ.

The majority of these Southern hemisphere pastors did see disciple-making as a process of growing to become like Christ, however, there were two common perceptions which must be recognized. First, many saw disciple-making as taking place in the "spiritual realm" rather than as holistic growth involving all aspects of life. Second, many described the process of shaping a disciple in individual terms rather than describing the role of the church or community. Twenty percent of the respondents viewed disciple-making as a form of methodology, such as Bible classes or study groups, mostly relying on formal and verbal communication. The focus was on the methodology rather than the outcome.

In this survey, sadly, 65.45 percent of the 900 pastors indicated that less than 50 percent of their church members are engaged in a disciple-making process, either being discipled by someone or discipling others. Of these pastors, about 30 percent stated that less than a quarter of their church members are engaged in *any* kind of disciple-making process.

The remaining third of the 900 evangelical pastors indicated that 50 percent or more of their church members are engaged in a disciple-making process. This means that only a third of these 900 churches have more than half of their church members intentionally pursuing personal growth into Christlikeness. This also means only a third of these evangelical churches have 50 percent or more of their church members obeying the Great Commission and making disciples.

Yet, if you are a North American pastor, perhaps you are not alarmed. Maybe those numbers don't sound too bad, because in North America the situation may be

## The One Thing — Disciple-Making

even worse. According to the Reveal study sponsored by Willow Creek Association, even among those American Christians who are "Christ-centered" (people who say "I love God more than anything else"), 25 percent do not pray daily, less than half read Scripture daily, less than 40 percent have six or more meaningful conversations with non-Christians in a year, and less than half are committed to mentoring or helping others grow spiritually.[2] Similarly unhappy news came from a Barna survey of 450 U.S. "born-again adults" asking, "What is the single most important thing you would like to accomplish in your life?" The top answer was to be good parents. Only 20 percent listed any answer related to their spiritual or faith condition, and none said "to be a committed follower of Jesus Christ or to make disciples."[3]

The early Ecclesia knew their mission was to surge forward toward the fulfillment and consummation of all things. They knew their mission was urgent. They saw their role in hastening the day of God, to "look forward to the day of God and speed its coming."[4]

We don't need to look at survey data to recognize that today's Christians generally do not have this type of urgency. In fact, quite a few of them are uncomfortable even talking about an urgent mission to save the lost. Our churches do not operate with this kind of energy, and the one mandate Jesus gave to us, to make disciples, is fading from our vocabulary.

But only when the Ecclesia is restored to its urgent mission, the Great Commission to make disciples of all nations, will the gates of Hades be overcome.

# The Mission of the Ecclesia: Make Disciples

Many Christians consider Jesus' redemptive work as only a means to *personal* reconciliation and fail to see it also as a means of reconciling all things to Him. Similarly, many Christians consider the Great Commission, the act of disciple-making, something we do as individuals. We send out individual missionaries, we individually share our faith with friends. But as we have stated earlier, it's the Ecclesia of Jesus Christ that is the unstoppable force of God. Power and authority has been given *to the Ecclesia*. Why? It is the Ecclesia that bears the Great Commission.

## The One Thing — Disciple-Making

In the book of Acts, Luke summarizes how Jesus spent the last 40 days of His earthly ministry. Acts 1:3 reports,

> After his suffering he showed himself to these men and gave many convincing proofs that he was alive. He appeared to them over a period of forty days and spoke about the kingdom of God.

Quite consistent with the other Gospels, Luke outlines three main tasks that Jesus engaged in and accomplished during those 40 days:

- Convincing His disciples that He had risen from the dead—the foundation of the new faith.[5]
- Helping His disciples to understand the "big picture," the kingdom of God—the ultimate goal.
- Entrusting to His disciples the Great Commission—the mission of the Ecclesia.

Within those 40 days, probably toward the end, Jesus gave the Great Commission to His disciples.[6] But He asked them to wait in Jerusalem before embarking on the Great Commission, until the Holy Spirit came upon them, which would mark the birth of the Ecclesia. This sequence suggests that the Great Commission was given to the Ecclesia, the new community that was built upon the foundation of the resurrection of Jesus Christ and empowered by the Holy Spirit. The same group of people who were called the disciples became the Ecclesia.

The Ecclesia has only one mission: to make disciples. In the Great Commission, Jesus did not command the Ecclesia to "engage in making disciples *and* also care for the poor," or to "make disciples *and* care for the creation," or to "make disciples *and* engage in the public square." This is because making disciples *includes* all of those aspects. The frame and ultimate goal of making disciples is the kingdom of God, the reign of God in individual lives and its reflections in family, community, and society. Bill Hull brings this all-encompassing aspect into focus:

When we follow Christ in discipleship, we grant permission for Christ to rule us. All that is included in Christ's rule—the fruit of the Spirit, the gifts of the Spirit, the guidance of the Spirit, the power of the Spirit—is present to influence the world around us. It is this quality in a person that makes transformation of culture possible.[7]

## Holistic Transformation through Holistic Disciple-Making

The broad-based transformation that can take place through a holistic approach to disciple-making is clearly illustrated in the East Indonesian ecclesia of Pastor Maykel Josef Ferdinand Pangkey.

Pastor Pangkey's ecclesia serves the Lewet village community, where most breadwinners are day laborers making $2 to $5 U.S. per day—on those days work is available. "They have to struggle to fulfill their basic needs," Pastor Pangkey remarks.

## Relentless HOPE

While reading Acts 6:1-7 about the seven men appointed to help administer help to the needy in the early Jerusalem ecclesia, Pastor Pangkey felt God telling him to do the same. *His people were familiar with the teachings of God's Word, but they had yet to follow Christ in action. The next step in their journeys as disciples would require doing the Word, not hearing it only.*[8]

So he encouraged the ecclesia to give and serve. Pastor Pangkey led the way in giving to buy food for distribution. Although help from his congregation came slowly, Pastor Pangkey kept urging his flock at every opportunity to become involved.

One by one, people began to respond. Some gave money. Others gave time to cook meals for those in the village who could no longer cook for themselves. Still others became cooking tutors for those who needed to learn how to cook after food was made available to them. And finally, the pastor was able to find seven people to take over the administration of this vital and practical ministry to families, within and without the ecclesia, in Lewet village.

## The One Thing — Disciple-Making

Many Christians in this ecclesia took the next steps on their journeys as disciples by simply putting their faith in action. Others in the village who are served by this ministry turned toward Christ and began their own journeys.

The disciple-making process is holistic in nature. Although Jesus did not commission the Ecclesia to eradicate poverty, He did ask the Ecclesia to make disciples. Through the disciple-making process, poverty can and should be eradicated. And in at least one place for one period of time it was eradicated.[9] Chris Sugden reflects,

> Christian maturity covers the whole of our humanity. We often reduce Christian maturity to the "spiritual" activities or regular prayer and Bible reading, personal evangelism, Christian service and active concerns for missionary society. We neglect goals and motives in career and job, attitude to community and social issues, involvement with others in fellowship and sharing, the practice of hospitality and the care of the underprivileged.[10]

Becoming a disciple is a holistic process. It takes place in community. The Great Commission to make disciples was not given to individual Christians, but to the Ecclesia. One can be born anywhere, but to grow holistically healthy, one needs a loving family. In much the same way, an individual Christian may be able to lead a person to accept Jesus Christ as Savior, but it will take the Ecclesia to make a true disciple. One Christian may be able to help other Christians grow in their spiritual journey, but an effective and holistic disciple-making process is best done in the context of a community of disciples—the Ecclesia.

## The Great Commission: Going, Baptizing, and Teaching

In order to understand what making disciples is all about, we need to look closely at the Great Commission. As recorded in Matthew 28:18-20, it says,

> All authority in heaven and on earth has been given to me. Therefore go and make disciples of all nations, baptizing

## The One Thing — Disciple-Making

them in the name of the Father and of the Son and of the Holy Spirit, and teaching them to obey everything I have commanded you. And surely I am with you always, to the very end of the age.

The imperative verb "make disciples" *(matheteuin)* in Mathew 28:19 defines the main action, the core content of the Great Commission. Matthew uses three participle verbs alongside the imperative verb; they are *poreuomai* (going), *baptizo* (baptizing), and *didasko* (teaching).

The first participle is *going*, and this sets the tone of the Great Commission. This word, *poreuomai*, means to travel or journey. Similarly, the disciple-making process is a journey, not a single event or moment of decision. This journey will lead each member of the Ecclesia to grow into Christlikeness. The journey of walking in Christ becomes an instrument of holistic witness through which others are drawn to Christ. Our journey is part of the disciple-making process for others. We are to "go" on that journey.

## Relentless HOPE

The audience of the Great Commission, those to whom we are *going*, is *ta ethnee*—all peoples and ethnic groups. Jesus did not limit the scope for disciple-making to candidates within the church building. In fact, the Great Commission assumes that disciple-making begins outside the church walls. Disciple-making is a transformation process bringing those far from Christ to closeness with Him. It is a process of helping people to move toward Christlikeness.

The second participle in the Great Commission is *baptizo*—"baptizing them in the name of the Father, the Son, and the Holy Spirit." Disciple-making begins before baptism. Nonetheless, baptism represents a significant milestone of belonging to, and entering into, a new community. The new believer's role in the disciple-making process changes from that of a recipient to that of a contributor, from being a customer to being an owner, from an audience to a bearer of the Great Commission.

The third participle is *didasko*—teaching them to obey or observe everything Jesus has taught them. The word implies a broad approach to learning, with a focus beyond just intellectual gains. The objective of the

## The One Thing — Disciple-Making

disciple-making process is not to accumulate knowledge of all the teachings of Jesus. If that were the case, the word *katecheo* (to inform, to instruct orally) might have been used. But the intended outcome of disciple-making is not only knowledge, it is the whole life affirmation of the Lordship of Christ—an attitude of obedience and submission to the reign and Lordship of Jesus Christ.

Disciple-making is thus aimed at creating a lifelong process of growth committed to the Lordship of Jesus Christ. It commits to an ongoing and intentional transformation into Christlikeness. Disciple-making is a dynamic journey of holistic personal growth in, with, and through the Ecclesia, for the purpose of the advancement of God's reign.

The death and resurrection of Jesus set human history on a new course. The kingdom of God has come, and the Ecclesia is now set to take the journey of turning the truth of the kingdom of God and the Lordship of Jesus Christ into reality for every individual, community, race, and nation. This is God's plan, and the Ecclesia's urgent mission.

The implications of this mission for our hurting world are nothing less than revolutionary. As the church makes authentic disciples, it develops a people who not only strengthen the church but also advance the reconciling work of God in our world.

## What Does It Mean to Be a Disciple?

The clear command of Jesus, His plan to restore this world, is to make disciples. Which leads to the important question, *what is a disciple?* Dallas Willard sets forth the classic definition of a disciple as a learner, an apprentice, and a practitioner.[11] Willard argues that being a disciple is "a quite definite and obvious kind of thing. To make a mystery of it is to misunderstand it."[12] He asserts, "You are somebody's disciple. You learned how to live from somebody else. There are no exceptions to this rule."[13] The question is not whether you are a disciple. The question is whose disciple are you? Who are you choosing to follow and be like?

Nearly all definitions of "disciple" emphasize the "student" aspect of the disciple as one who "learns." Yet the intention of a disciple to follow and obey Jesus as

Lord involves more than intellectual knowledge. Such intentions are forged in a complex mix of knowledge, desires, and attitudes, patterning of behaviors and the working of the Holy Spirit. The disciple's intention to be like Jesus flows from an orientation of the will—that executive center of human action. The disciple's intent is not a state of permanency. Rather, in the daily process of putting off the old self, the disciple is continually growing in the strength and consistency of their intentions to follow Jesus and, with increasing frequency, those intentions are proven genuine in their actions. And as we are about to see, one can only grow as he or she helps others to grow.

# Disciples Make Disciples

Many things have been written about disciple-making and what it means to be a disciple. Those things do not need to be recounted here. We do need to affirm one of the characteristics of a disciple: *disciples make disciples*. One of the key points at which Jesus calls His disciples is found in Matthew 4:19: "Come, follow me," Jesus said, "and I will make you fishers of men."

## Relentless HOPE

Jesus calls His disciples to follow Him and promises that He will change them in such a way that they themselves will become fishers of men, or in other words, disciple-makers. Jesus indicates that following Him, living in obedient alignment to His way of life, will transform the follower into a leader. The disciple will make disciples. Jesus will do this as an act of His own work in and through the disciple's obedience.

> **The radiant evidence of the love of God in our lives should inspire. Humility and joyful self-sacrifice should mystify. Forgiveness should unravel the skeptic, and purpose-filled hope should be a magnet drawing those without hope into a life-revolutionizing discovery.**

Can one be a disciple and not make other disciples? Can one become a Christian and not become a

## The One Thing — Disciple-Making

bearer of the Great Commission? If obedience is the mark of a disciple, then the answer is no.

And yet we see churches crowded with nondisciple-making Christians. Can one be baptized, belong to Jesus, and become a member of the Ecclesia, and not engage in the process of making disciples? The Bible is very clear, the answer is no. This matter of being a disciple-making Ecclesia is of paramount importance. This is God's Plan A. This is the only way that God is going to change, to redeem, to transform, to restore this world.

Perhaps that blunt claim is a bit intimidating. We have basically laid out two simple statements. There is no such thing as a "nondisciple Christian." And disciples must make disciples. In fact, they can't help but do so.

These statements are intimidating partially because it is common to assume that making disciples requires programs, mentoring, evangelism, and the like. Such methods are important and can be part of the disciple-making process, but to take such a limited view of disciple-making would be frightening. We would wring our hands wondering how to invent a strategy that will entice, persuade, argue, or otherwise compel others to give themselves to Jesus.

## Relentless HOPE

Why do golf courses around the world suddenly become full with golfers after an incredible golfer plays in the Masters? Why do children run outside to play football (soccer) after seeing the World Cup on television? Why does listening to your friend speaking fluently in another language make you want to learn that language? The answer is simple. Inspiration.

Disciple-making should be like that. The radiant evidence of the love of God in our lives should inspire. Humility and joyful self-sacrifice should mystify. Forgiveness should unravel the skeptic, and purpose-filled hope should be a magnet drawing those without hope into a life-revolutionizing discovery. Our abiding in the vine, our bearing the fruit of the Spirit, and our living in the life that is truly life[14] creates the inspiring draw upon the souls of those without Christ. Disciples make disciples. In fact, they cannot help but do so.

Jesus commissioned the Ecclesia to make authentic disciples. We are to raise up a people who not only claim His name, who not only follow in the crowd, but who are continuously growing in their conformity to Christ and making other disciples as they go. That was

## The One Thing — Disciple-Making

what He asked us to do. That was His plan for us and our world:

Go make disciples. Go make little Christs. Go make servant leaders. Go make miracle workers. Go make people who will forgive the same offense 490 times over. Go make people who weep for the suffering of others. Go make people who lose their lives in order to find them. Go make joy radiators. Go make peacemakers. Go make people who speak the truth in love, who face injustice with courage, who lift up the hurting, who see a man on the street beaten, robbed, and left for dead and pay for his lodging and medical needs. Go make disciples. That's the simple plan. That is the only thing He has asked of us.

All that is necessary for the healing of everything from broken marriages to the end of global poverty is found in this simple strategy: *be disciples who make disciples*.

# FOUR
# CHILDREN AS
# Disciples

# Relentless HOPE

Is it really worth the time and effort to disciple children? Are children actually ready to become Christ-followers before they become adults?

The Bible presents children and youth as partners in advancing God's mission—now, and in the future. Children may even have a greater capacity than adults to worship, depend, and trust. These are key attributes of a disciple. A quick examination of the Bible shows that God engages children in many of the same ways that He works with us as adults. Consider these stories from the Bible of children advancing God's kingdom:

- God used the counsel of Naaman's young servant girl in 2 Kings 5 to bring about the healing of Naaman's leprosy. Naaman was an influential leader whose healing prompted him to say, "Now I know that there is no God in all the world except in Israel."

- 1 Samuel 3 records that God spoke directly to Samuel as a child and used him to share a vision with Eli.

## Children as Disciples

- Josiah became the king of Israel when he was just 8, and by the time he was 16, he began to seek the Lord and serve Him wholeheartedly. He purged Israel of idols and brought about a spiritual revival. 2 Chronicles 34:33 says of this boy king, "He had all who were present in Israel serve the Lord their God. As long as he lived, they did not fail to follow the Lord, the God of their fathers."

- 1 Samuel 17 recounts how God used David, as a young and unknown boy, to defeat the giant warrior Goliath and save the Israelites from the Philistines when he defeated Goliath.

- The Book of Esther tells how God used Esther, a brave teenage girl in captivity, to save the Israelites from genocide.

- As told in John 6, Jesus used the loaves and fishes of one small boy to feed the crowd of 5,000.

- God Himself entered the world through Mary, a teenage girl.

It's this simple: God cherishes children and engages them to do great things for His glory. How, then, can we deny children the opportunity to be disciples of Jesus Christ?

## Spiritual Formation and Disciple-Making in Childhood

Given the choice of when to begin working in a person's life, would we rather begin with an insecure and angry adult or with a child yet to be inflicted with much of the damage of our sin-stained world?

The forming and growth of our spirits begins in early childhood. The words of Psalm 22:9-10 reflect David's experience: "Yet you [God] brought me out of the womb; you made me trust in you even at my mother's breast. From birth I was cast upon you; from my mother's womb you have been my God."

As Dallas Willard points out, we are first disciples of our parents, playmates, and teachers.[1] In childhood, we may be shaped by lies or by truth. The spirit may germinate in the soil of loving relationships or may strain to break through the concrete of anger and jealousies. And we will become like those who serve as our examples—angry or gracious.

Ask any professional in early child development about those events that are most formative for a human and you will hear them describe the importance of "mother-child bonding." This relationship can build trust, security, belonging, identity, and the experience of being loved. From that foundation of safety, a child finds courage to explore his or her world. From the security of that relationship, the child builds a foundational understanding of what it means to trust others.

> **It's this simple: God cherishes children and engages them to do great things for His glory.**

Consider the alternative. Babies who are neglected—even when their physical needs are met—suffer detachment, ambivalence, and, in serious cases, may even die. The stage is set for insecurity, anger, and a re-expression of those hatreds they have experienced later in life. (Not to say that Jesus cannot rescue and reshape that soul—He has the power to buy us back from whatever evil has captured us no matter how early in life the wounds are inflicted. But there will be much pain and suffering and mistrust to work through.)

Life's experiences shape all of us; by intimacy or neglect, by insults or praise, by security or violence, by belonging or rejection, by learning or darkness. Clearly, childhood, even very early childhood, is a critical stage of life in which to join God in building Christlike people.

# The 4/14 Window

Indeed, childhood is a critical window of opportunity in the disciple-making process. Here we hope to offer a perspective that will shape the future of holistic ministry and integral mission as it relates to children.

In 1995, Compassion International leaders were discussing the 10/40 Window and wrestling with how to communicate the importance of children in mission. They coined the term "the 4/14 Window,"[2] which was first introduced at a conference in Colorado Springs,

## Children as Disciples

Colorado, and published by Compassion Program Director Dan Brewster in 1996.

The concept of the 4/14 Window was ignited by data from Bryant Myers, now at Fuller Seminary, whose research demonstrated that "85 percent of people who make a decision for Christ, do so between the ages of 4 and 14."[3] These findings were confirmed for U.S. children by George Barna in 2003. He reported that "the probability of someone embracing Jesus as his or her Savior was 32 percent for those between the ages of 5 and 12; 4 percent for those in the 13- to 18-age range; and 6 percent for people 19 and older. In other words, if people do not embrace Jesus Christ as their Savior before they reach their teenage years, the chance of their doing so at all is slim."[4] Similarly, a recent Willow Creek *Reveal* study reports that growing up in a church is the leading reason people begin exploring Christianity.[5] In fact, the vast majority of Christians in our churches today forged their lifelong commitment to Jesus during their childhood or adolescent years.

Although this insight was first reported some years ago (1996), we are only beginning to see its implications impacting mission strategies. Those implications are well articulated in *Future Impact: Connecting Child, Church, and Mission* by Dan Brewster.[6]

Discussions of ministry to children often lead to questions about a child's readiness to make such a commitment or to theological issues such as the age of accountability. Here we would like to avoid those controversies. Instead, let us reconsider the foundation we have established for the disciple-making process and spiritual formation: relationship.

The disciple-making process can begin before a person "knows" Jesus or has intention to follow Him. Consider again John the Baptist who leapt in his mother's womb when he "met" Jesus, demonstrating some form of precognitive communion with the Holy Spirit.[7] Disciple-making does not begin at the point of accepting Jesus as Savior, but is a process of being introduced to Jesus Christ.

# When Does Disciple-Making Begin?

When Christ commands us to go and make disciples, we must ask ourselves, "To whom should we go?"

We often think of *where* we are to go—to all nations and even to the ends of the earth. But have you ever thought of "all people" not in terms of geography but in terms of age? Is there any limit to when, in human development, the Spirit is able to begin the process of making a disciple? Does the Spirit require a certain level of cognitive or emotional development in order to begin this work?

Very often, descriptions of disciple-making place a heavy emphasis on cognitive motivation, like Willard's: "one who has firmly decided to learn from [Jesus] how to lead his or her life."[8] Definitions of disciple-making that describe things such as "firmly deciding" or "learning" naturally lead us to adult-focused strategies for disciple-making. Adults, after all, are the ones who have the cognitive development necessary for learning and firmly deciding.

If one sees the disciple-making process as primarily cognitive, then one teaches and instructs. And, no doubt, one would see children as having limited capacity as disciples due to their limited capacities for "learning" and understanding the truths of Scripture. In contrast, if one sees disciple-making as primarily developing Christlike behavior, then one models and coaches such behavior. In that case, children can certainly learn behavior, and many parenting strategies focus on behavioral outcomes.

But if one sees disciple-making as not just a behavioral or cognitive change, but foundationally as forming a relationship, then one seeks to make an introduction—to create an encounter. If Truth is a person, then relationship is the center of disciple-making. The priority becomes learning to recognize the Truth and begin communicating with Him (prayer). If this is the case, then children may even have advantages over adults due to their unique capacity for trust, faith, dependency, and communication.

To be clear, we are distinguishing *being a disciple* from the process of *disciple-making* (the Spirit-enabled work of leading others toward Christ). One cannot be a disciple without intentionally surrendering the personal will to the Divine will. We "choose" to follow, to obey, to be like the Master. However, a person can be *led toward* Christlikeness, even prior to their intention to follow Jesus. A *disciple* has acted upon their intention to follow Jesus, but *disciple-making* is a process of leading people, including children, toward Christlikeness and may begin before that person forms intentions to become a disciple.

Before Jesus gave Peter's fishing business a miraculous economic windfall, Peter had no intention of following Jesus. Afterward, Peter left everything to follow Jesus—and became a disciple at that moment.[9] Yet Jesus began making a disciple of Peter the moment He got into Peter's boat and asked him, as stated in Luke 5:3, to "put out a little from shore." Jesus began the "disciple-making" (*matheteuin*) of Peter even before Peter recognized Jesus as the Christ. As Peter followed Jesus, his intentions for following and his obedience grew in depth and strengthened in consistency. Yet the depth and consistency of Peter's commitment to Jesus wavered. Even after years of following and learning from Jesus, even after witnessing the miracles, the transfiguration, and even after taking a brief walk on water, Peter's consistent intention to be Jesus' disciple faltered. Jesus began making a disciple of Peter well before Peter's confession of Jesus as the Christ, and Jesus was continuing to make a disciple of Peter even after Peter's denial. Disciple-making is a process and a journey and along that journey there is more than one point of "decision" (intention) in which the disciple becomes a disciple.

To further emphasize the point, it was *after* Jesus healed the two blind men that they chose to follow Him.[10] The process of leading others toward Christlikeness (disciple-making) may begin before they have any knowledge of who Christ is or hold any intention to follow His way.

Disciple-making does not *begin* at the moment a person confesses Jesus as Lord. It begins before that and extends throughout the life of that person as it moves them toward Christlikeness. Therefore, the disciple-making process can, and must, include children.

# An Integrated Perspective of Spiritual Formation in Children

Human identity is an integrated whole, encompassing body, mind, social connectedness, and spirit. God desires to restore our whole identity. Therefore, the disciple-making process for children should not address only one aspect, but *every* aspect of their being.

An integrated program for spiritual formation of children would surround a child with experiences of Christ's love. As the child grows, they should experience the love and nurture of others and be protected from hates and exploitations. They should be encouraged to recognize God in their midst through wonder and awe at His work. They should be taught about the truths of Scripture, learning its stories, memorizing God's promises, and relating those to their experience of life.

They should be well nourished physically, protected from disease, and allowed to play, that they might grow in "stature" as Jesus did. A child who is too hungry to focus her mind will not only fail to be interested in cognitive instruction about God's provision, she will harbor a profound skepticism about such "teaching" as it contrasts to her own experience.

This is the approach to take toward disciple-making with children. It ensures the child's physical environment allows them to thrive, having enough to eat, living in a safe environment. It strives to create a social environment around them that teaches them of their value and protects them from wrongs. It teaches them about God's love through Bible classes, models Christlike behavior to them, and shows them Christ's love through relationship.

This integrated approach to disciple-making is crucial, as God desires to restore every aspect of our being. All of it is disciple-making. No part in isolation is sufficient, nor is one aspect "more important" than another. As the Ecclesia works together to make whole disciples, these young people will be—as they have been—God's agents to transform this world.

## Children and Youth as Transforming Agents

Children and youth have played significant roles in the great historical revivals of John Wesley, Jonathan Edwards, D. L. Moody, the French Huguenots, and others. And God is still using children today to be His agents of mission.

Consider Patricia, a 12-year-old girl living in the slum community of Santa Mesa in the Philippines.

## Children as Disciples

This community is known to be a breeding ground for thieves, criminals, and prostitutes. Patricia saw how the children of her neighborhood were rowdy, dirty, and disrespectful, so she started teaching 5- to 10-year-olds the Bible. She gathers them together once a week and tells them about Jesus. She says she doesn't want them to grow up to be criminals, but to know about Jesus.

> **We believe that the next generation, children, are vital to restoring the Ecclesia to her great mission of making disciples and transforming this world**

Pronchai is a 15-year-old boy from an isolated and minority tribal group in Thailand. He moved to the city for schooling, where drugs are far too familiar to children and where bad environmental practices are used, such as forest burning. Pronchai has shown himself to be a leader and become the initiator of several community activities, such as environmental causes and drug prevention initiatives. He teaches youth about protecting

## Relentless HOPE

trees and has organized tree-planting events. He has also worked to educate youth about the danger of drugs. As a result, his school received the "Clean School without Drugs" award from the Princess of Thailand.

These modern day examples of youth being agents of God's mission to transform the world around them are inspiring but not uncommon. In both the Northern and Southern Ecclesia, we have witnessed thousands of young people living out their faith and advancing the reconciling and healing work of God in their communities. There is a new movement of churches all over the world who are awaking to the potential of children—and not just in the future, but now. According to the January-February 2008 *Ministry Today*, this is igniting a spiritual revolution in these churches. Children aren't just coming to church to be entertained. In response to the opportunity and challenge they've been given, they come to worship and contribute and be equipped.

We must also see the powerful truth of their future potential to carry forth generational change. Scripture teaches us, in Proverbs 22:6, to "train a child in the way he should go, and when he is old he will not turn from it." Such training is actually disciple-making;

that *didasko* type of training, which holistically equips young apprentices of Jesus.

We believe that the next generation, children, are vital to restoring the Ecclesia to her great mission of making disciples and transforming this world. But we aren't the only ones who realize this.

# The Adversary

To discuss disciple-making or spiritual formation in childhood without considering the forces opposed to Jesus would leave us vulnerable and naive. We might operate on the assumption that there is little urgency. We might act as if the next generation of Christ-followers simply awaits our instruction while peacefully eating their cereal or rice. Nothing could be further from the truth. They are already "under instruction."

*The forces of darkness are not hesitating to act in childhood.* The enemy seems to recognize childhood as a critical and vulnerable stage during which he might destroy what God loves. And so that enemy who seeks to "steal, kill, and destroy" mounts a full assault on

### Relentless HOPE

children as early as possible, as ferociously as possible and as deceptively as possible.

The host of human sin, with greed and ambition leading the way, has constructed societies and systems that neglect, marginalize, and exploit our youngest, most vulnerable citizens. Nearly 24,000 children die every day from preventable causes.[11] Nearly 100 million children are not in school because of poverty. An estimated 1 million children are coerced into the sex trade every year. The assault on children is ruthless—and no doubt our enemy is pleased.

Poverty is only one strategy of our enemy. While millions of children are robbed of opportunity to realize their God-given potential due to the threat of poverty, there are millions more who are hammered into a false identity through the strategies of consumerism. The average American child spends 4 hours a day watching TV and will see 20,000 30-second TV ads per year. They witness 8,000 murders on TV by the time they finish elementary school.[12]

Corporations are spending billions of dollars on "youth marketing" strategies to build brand loyalty

## Children as Disciples

among children as young as two years old. That money saturates children with lies. "You must buy this product in order to be happy. You must buy this product in order to be accepted by your friends. You must buy in order to be important." And thus whole societies of "good" consumers are grown from the soil of these lies.

If corporations can recognize the strategic importance of children then we, as the people of God, the leaders of the church, must not be naive. We must fight for the hearts of the next generation of Christ-followers. If the enemy recognizes the key role of children, then we, too, must realize their significance in the kingdom of God. We beg Christian leaders to recognize the importance of children.

Our hope is that in the next century of holistic mission we, the disciples of Jesus, will shake off our disoriented view of who is the greatest. Our hope is that we will see the importance of children. That we will protect them, learn from them, and become more effective at introducing them to Jesus.

**The Ecclesia must realize that the disciple-making process can begin with children.** Children need

## Relentless HOPE

to be nurtured and cared for holistically. And when we develop their abilities, promise, and potential, God works in them as an incredible force to bring His kingdom to this world.

# FIVE
# GLOBAL CONNECTIONS, LOCAL
# Relationships

## Relentless HOPE

So we know *what* the Plan A mission is: make disciples. We know *how* to fulfill the Plan A mission: through the holistic disciple-making of all people, especially in ministry to children. We know *who* Jesus Christ built to be Plan A: the Ecclesia.

But one element is still missing, one we would say is of utmost importance as the Ecclesia seeks to transform this world: connecting the global body of Christ, the Northern Christians and Southern Christians, in order to best mobilize all our resources in this mission.

We would embody the picture given us in Ephesians 2:19-22:

> Consequently, you are no longer foreigners and aliens, but fellow citizens with God's people and members of God's household, built on the foundation of the apostles and prophets, with Christ Jesus himself as the chief cornerstone. In him the whole building is joined together and rises to become a holy temple in the Lord. And in him you too are being built together

to become a dwelling in which God lives by His Spirit.

The question is, *How do we best join together to become that dwelling, optimizing both our global connections and local relationships?*

At least part of the answer is found in the networking of the Early Church.

# The Cross-Cultural Spread of the Good News

We've seen the example of the impact the Early Church had on the world around them. In the power of the Holy Spirit, these believers witnessed verbally, and also through signs and wonders. They committed themselves to prayer. They committed themselves to the teaching of the apostles. They ate together. Yes, that matters.

And these believers, the first Ecclesia, began to recognize and respond to the many needs of others. They sold their possessions. They healed people of physical disabilities. No one was in need.

The community around them watched this emerging fellowship. All who saw it were impressed. Acts 2:47 reports that the believers were "enjoying the favor of all the people." Every day more people were joining their numbers.

But, of course, the enemy wasn't pleased by any of this. Religious leaders launched a violent campaign to stamp out this new sect. The early believers were scattered. The apostles stayed in Jerusalem, continuing to move in great power. And the scattered believers, the Diaspora, were unstoppable. They courageously witnessed to distant communities. The violence and oppression only fueled the movement, spreading the joy of the good news and the power of a truly healing ministry. New communities of believers, new ecclesia, were born and grew in places as far away as Phoenicia, Cyprus, and Antioch.

It was in Antioch that these pioneering and power-filled believers began to witness to Gentiles. Antioch was a very important center in the Roman Empire, a crossroads for much of the Asian region. Out of this center came an emerging wealthy church that was now willing and able to support the people of the Way. Their integrity was noted by the people of Antioch, who—for the first time anywhere—called followers of Jesus "Christians." The cross-cultural spread of the good news was ignited.

The church in Jerusalem sent support to this group through Barnabas. In the Antioch ecclesia, Barnabas "saw the evidence of the grace of God."[1] The gospel was visible. It was alive in the Ecclesia. Barnabas quickly realized he needed more support and went to Tarsus looking for a man by the name of Saul. Together they witnessed and ministered in Antioch to both Jews and Greeks. The Ecclesia grew in depth and numbers.

# Cross-Cultural Generosity

It was in Antioch that God revealed to His people that a severe famine was imminent. The believers in Antioch responded. They decided to do all they could to help their brothers and sisters in Judea.[2]

# Relentless HOPE

Acts 2:45 says that as soon as the church was born, the evidence of generosity and sharing had been amazing: "Selling their possessions and goods, they gave to anyone as he had need." Now in Antioch the generosity spilled over cultural borders as a result of their new faith. The Ecclesia had already demonstrated generosity within a local community, and in Antioch the power of that generosity broke across cultural boundaries. Community solidarity took on a new meaning. Community of tribe or geography or language did not stand as a barricade within the community of Christ.

Perhaps the believers in Antioch felt a sense of gratitude to those who brought the gospel to them. For the transfer of financial resources from Antioch to Jerusalem was not the first act of generosity between ecclesia. The Jerusalem believers who brought the gospel to Antioch had fled persecution, narrowly escaping arrest and violence. They had lost their jobs and homes. They had become disconnected from extended family and friends. It would have been quite understandable for such people, having experienced the trauma of persecution, to "lay low." But they didn't. They courageously shared the gospel in Antioch and carried forward the

Great Commission. In doing so, they shared a resource far greater than finances.

This act of giving established an important precedent. The generosity of the Antioch Christians demonstrated a cross-cultural solidarity, a unity found in Christ, *between* different ecclesia—not just within an ecclesia.

When practical, physical needs arise, each ecclesia should mobilize according to her ability, as the church in Antioch did in response to the need. This giving is not only an act of worship, but also an incredible witness. The witnessing of the early believers was not mere talk. It was witnessing in action. The famine went on for many years, and it became a pattern and passion of the apostle Paul to mobilize the ecclesia in one location to help bring an offering on behalf of believers who were in need elsewhere.

## What Do We Have to Give?

Is this just about those with material possessions giving them away, and the recipients being grateful? Is

# Relentless HOPE

that God's plan for the kingdom—some to learn to be generous givers and some to be gracious recipients? As we see from the example of Antioch and Jerusalem, in the kingdom of God, every believer and ecclesia has something to give.

Consider the Macedonians, a group of churches in the region of Macedonia. Paul had a strong sense of need to raise money for the struggling church in Judea where they were facing a serious shortage of food. He was expecting a gift from the Corinthians, a wealthy church. But Paul was surprised by the Macedonians—they had a strong desire to give even though they were themselves in extreme poverty. In fact, the Macedonian church urgently pleaded with Paul for the privilege of giving. He described the situation as follows in 2 Corinthians 8:2: "Out of the most severe trial, [the Macedonians'] overflowing joy and their extreme poverty welled up in rich generosity."

Many of us read this passage and ask, probably like Paul, "What did the Macedonians have to give?" Surely they had very little in the way of material goods. Still, they gave as much as they were able and "even beyond their ability." Paul says that the Macedonians first gave themselves to the Lord, and it was their complete attitude of dependence on God that gave them a perspective that is often difficult for the resource-rich. From their utter dependency, they no longer saw their situation from an earthly perspective, but they instead had the perspective of all they had available to them through the riches and promises of God. The result: overflowing joy and a rich generosity that came from deep within.

## Corinth and the True Life

Corinth was an educational center and its population was well-to-do. The group of believers in Corinth had much to offer. They excelled, as Scripture says in 2 Corinthians 8:7, "in faith, in speech, in knowledge, and in complete earnestness." But it seems that they lacked excellence in the grace of giving.

When Paul first told the believers in Corinth of the physical needs in Judea, they had been eager to share. But a year later, they weren't following up on their promises. Although the Corinthians abounded in gifts, it seems that they lacked the understanding that all gifts are given to be used for a greater purpose. We are blessed so that we can be a blessing to others. Holding on to more than enough creates a false confidence for the believer and hinders God's plans for blessing others through it.

In contrast, the Macedonians had no abundance to lean on, but they had learned to depend on God completely. They caught the vision of reaching out to another and were focused on supporting that need. We can all look inside ourselves and our own ecclesia and find needs. But too much inward focus on our own needs will never allow us to experience the joy of giving to others. There is real joy in being able to witness, bring glory to God and the good news of the gospel to others, while responding also to their specific needs.

As you look at your own ecclesia, which do you more resemble—Macedonia or Corinth? Paul's advice to the rich in 1 Timothy 6:17-19 is so vital to us today who resemble Corinth more than Macedonia:

> Command those who are rich in this present world not to be arrogant nor to put their hope in wealth, which is so uncertain,

but to put their hope in God, who richly provides us with everything for our enjoyment. Command them to do good, to be rich in good deeds, and to be generous and willing to share. In this way they will lay up treasure for themselves as a firm foundation for the coming age, so that they may take hold of the life that is truly life.

Real generosity and an attitude of sharing free us to "take hold of the life that is truly life." This true life, or as Jesus puts it, the kingdom of heaven, is where we become more and more like Christ. God's purpose is for all of us to live this true life.

# The Connector

Paul understood that the Ecclesia would grow in this true life as they reached out to the needs of others. He pushed for the Ecclesia to come together in providing for the needs of one another. He flourished in the role he played in connecting the Ecclesia together in order to achieve the things they could not achieve on their own.

So what was Paul's role? As a messenger of the gospel, he was passionate about building up the local ecclesia. To do so, he spent much of his time traveling between them and, through exhortation and encouragement, he ministered and reached out to their complete needs. Paul was a connector of churches for the broader purpose of expanding the kingdom.

He connected the Macedonians to Corinthians. Both of them faced serious challenges. The ecclesia in Macedonia suffered from extreme poverty. They probably watched as their families and communities suffered from malnutrition. The Corinthian ecclesia suffered from something not as visible but possibly more deadly. They had a heart problem: their self-sufficiency led to self-confidence, and then to idolatry. They were too self-absorbed to follow through on their commitment to help others.

The Corinthians could have really used the faith the Macedonians seemed to have. The Macedonians could really use what the Corinthians had. In fact, the combining of the gifts of both ecclesia would create a much healthier body. Both of these ecclesia were willing to minister to the needs of another ecclesia. What they needed was a connector. Paul served as a ligament, along with other traveling church leaders, that connected the first-generation global church. Once connected, the Ecclesia could reach a new level as the strong and healthy body of Christ. As Paul had written the ecclesia in Ephesus, "From him the whole body, joined and held together by every supporting ligament, grows and builds itself up in love, as each part does its work."[3]

We need modern-day Pauls to link the local ecclesia and play an ongoing support role between them, but who are themselves also deeply involved in a local ecclesia. So who are our modern-day Pauls? They are people of God, part of a local ecclesia, who are called to use their plenty to minister to, strengthen, and mobilize the broader Ecclesia. This might be in the context of working within a particular denomination or association, like the Willow Creek Association, providing leadership and support to the expansion of the Ecclesia through church planters and developers of local pastors and lay leaders.

Maybe you are a member of a local ecclesia who is called to serve in a ministry whose mission is to equip, support, and minister alongside the local ecclesia in fulfilling the Great Commission. Many of these ministries, like Compassion, are called "parachurch organizations." They are not the Ecclesia, but, as people of God, they exist to fulfill the Great Commission through the *strengthening* of the worldwide Ecclesia to fulfill its mandate of making disciples.[4]

Those of us in parachurch ministries have a key role to play. God has given our ministries unique gifts to use to further the kingdom. Important questions for all of us who are playing that role must include, "To what extent do we allow the Ecclesia to hold us accountable? To what extent do we see ourselves subservient to the local ecclesia? To what extent do we recognize that our role is to be the bridesmaids helping to prepare the bride of Christ?"

The Bridegroom, Jesus, is coming back for His bride, and the bridesmaids will be judged. While we all wait for that day, we are called to make disciples. Let us be committed to supporting the local ecclesia in its mandate, for we, too, will be held accountable.

# In Complete Unity

Sometimes talking about unity within the global Church is met with skepticism. But how can that be when unity among His followers was the prayer of Jesus Himself?

> I pray also for those who will believe in me through their message, that all of them may be one, Father, just as you are in me and I am in you. May they also be in us so that the world may believe that you have sent me. I have given them the glory that you gave me, that they may be one as we are one: I in them and you in me. May they be brought to complete unity to let the world know that you sent me and have loved them even as you have loved me.[5]

Jesus' prayer for the believers, for the global body of believers, was that they would become one, as He and the Father are one. That they be brought to complete unity. Not only for their sakes, but to let the world know that Jesus was sent by the Father and that the Father loves them even as He loved Jesus.

As Jesus' prayer indicates, *unity within and between the Ecclesia is one of the key aspects of attracting the lost and making disciples*. Like never before in church history, Christians have an opportunity in the 21st century to draw from the multitude of gifts, resources, and talents amongst the global body of believers. The world we live in today allows many of us to travel great distances. Today's global connectedness is unparalleled in history. Yet just because we are connected doesn't mean we speak the same language. The unity that Jesus prayed for requires more than airplanes and the Internet. The Holy Spirit must align the thoughts and actions of the Ecclesia.

This connectedness may be a part of God's providence in helping the Ecclesia complete the task before her. Yet it demands a connection that links us to a common cause and common language. The message and practice of making disciples must be the language in and among the Ecclesia. The world and its needs, the fate of the lost, have been brought to the forefront in both the global South and North. And God has said, "Go!"

What can an ecclesia offer as connecting points? From now on, nothing is impossible. Every ecclesia can and should bring something to the broader body. Some may give through prayer and financial support. As the Psalmist says in Psalm 112:9, the godly man "has scattered abroad his gifts to the poor." And as we have seen, without those scattered gifts much of the Early Church might not have survived.

> **For the Ecclesia to work in partnership with one another is not simply a good model, it is the kingdom design for a healthy body**

For many Northern Christians, the experience of worshiping alongside Southern Christians often instills a longing for the warmth and vibrancy of that worship when they return home. Christians living in the oppressive context of poverty need godly stewardship from those whom God has granted financial resources. Christians living in the oppressive context of consumerism and postmodernism need the witness of faith

## Relentless HOPE

and inspiring examples of perseverance that Southern Christians often bring.

We all can learn from and encourage one another, just like the Corinthians and Macedonians. Our churches in the global North need the Church in Africa and Asia and Latin America. The churches in Africa, Asia and Latin America need the Church of the North. And churches within a particular region also need each other. For the Ecclesia to work in partnership with one another is not simply a good model, it is the kingdom design for a healthy body.

The world needs the life-giving Ecclesia, committed to making disciples by reaching out and responding to all the needs of the lost and the hurting. The world needs to see the unity of the believers as we live, relate, and minister together. The beauty of our Lord is that He knew we would not find all of the gifts in one place, but He has scattered abroad His gifts to the poor. We must come together as the body of Christ to draw on all of God's gifts. All the world is watching as we come together to bring the kingdom of God and transform this world. In his stirring address at the 1910

## Global Connections, Local Relationships

World Missionary Conference in Edinburgh, Indian church leader V. S. Azariah utilized both Ephesians 3 and 1 Corinthians 13 that was nothing less than visionary regarding the need for a globally connected Church, both in strategy and relationship:

> The exceeding riches of the glory of Christ can be fully realised not by the Englishman, the American, and the Continental alone, nor by the Japanese, the Chinese, and the Indians by themselves – but by all working together, worshipping together, and learning together the Perfect Image of our Lord and Christ. It is only "with all the Saints" that we can "comprehend the love of Christ which passeth knowledge, that we might be filled with all the fullness of God." This will be possible only from spiritual friendships between the two races. We ought to be willing to learn from one another and to help one another.

## Relentless HOPE

> Through all the ages to come the Indian Church will rise up in gratitude to attest the heroism and self-denying labours of the missionary body. You have given your goods to feed the poor. You have given your bodies to be burned. We also ask for *love*. Give us FRIENDS![6]

The Ecclesia is commanded to go, but she dare not go alone. This is a call for humble partnerships leading to mutual strengthening and to the advance of the reign of God. May Jesus' prayer for unity be answered not through consensus on details of doctrine but through common devotion to Jesus, the unique Son of God. May the Ecclesia learn from each other and be diligent in her efforts to *be* a people of good news to a hurting world.

This is a call to focus on the next generation, our sons and our daughters and their peers. We must stop seeking short-term solutions to global issues and recognize that generational change is required. We must recognize the strategic and scriptural importance of children and correct our disoriented view of greatness to raise the next generation in the Way of Christ.

> **The solutions to global poverty are not awaiting scientific discovery, they are waiting to grow up.**

The solutions to global poverty are not awaiting scientific discovery, they are waiting to grow up. Children, if protected and given opportunity, will become change agents developing their communities and nations. Developing authentic disciples transforms the larger community with healing and forgiveness. The Ecclesia *is* the hope of the world.

This is a call to the people of God who are organized in parachurch agencies or denominational structures to equip and empower the Ecclesia, the local congregation, for her commission. Do nothing to hinder or compete with her. Enable her effectiveness in holistic ministry and build her reputation among the nations that people may turn to her and discover Jesus in the midst of local, dynamic kingdom community.

This is a call for every local church, every ecclesia, to rediscover her commission and hold fast to the vision of the triumphant bride of Christ prevailing against the gates of hell. Resolve to make authentic disciples of Jesus. Lead *all* people of *every* age wherever they are in life into the Way of Jesus.

Ecclesia *is* the great hope of our ailing world. She is God's Plan A. She is the divine entity empowered by the Holy Spirit, manifesting *agape* love, equipped with heavenly authority, and placed in this world. The bar may be fearfully high, but the rightful place of ecclesia is at the center of God's plan—and thus of human history.

## About Compassion International

Compassion International is a Christian holistic child-development ministry working to release over one million children from poverty. More than 50 years of child-development experience have shaped Compassion's understanding of children and childhood as critically important for individual, family, community and national transformation.

## The Compassion Difference

- **Christ Centered.** Each child has an opportunity to hear the gospel in an age-appropriate and culturally relevant way.
- **Child Focused.** Engaging each child as a complete person, we protect and nurture each child in all aspects of their growth.
- **Church Based.** We partner with local Christian churches to equip them for ministry with children.
- **Committed to Integrity.** We are dedicated to delivering excellent programs with complete integrity.

## Compassion's Mission Statement

In response to the Great Commission, Compassion International exists as an advocate for children, to release them from their spiritual, economic, social and physical poverty and enable them to become responsible and fulfilled Christian adults.

# Relentless HOPE

## Publishing at Compassion

God nurtures a very special relationship with the poor and the oppressed. Those without the power to change their lot. Nowhere do forces of poverty and oppression do more harm than in the lives of the world's poorest children.

That's why Compassion publishes books to help Christians understand the destruction poverty inflicts. To see the potential of children crushed in its grip. And to unleash the overwhelming power of the Church to free children—one by one, village by village, nation by nation.

When Christians spend themselves in the development of a child, they are invested in the purpose of God. These books inform that cause and inspire action. These books enable the Church to experience God's call of releasing children from poverty in Jesus' name.

## The Blue Corner

Every book that rolls off the press through Publishing at Compassion bears a symbol of God's intent. Our blue corner points back to Leviticus 23:22.

> When you reap the harvest of your land, don't reap the corners of your field or gather the gleanings. Leave them for the poor and the foreigners. (MSG)

This symbol is reminder to leave a "corner of our lives" on behalf of the poor.

# NOTES

## Introduction

1. Cited by Brian Stanley, *The World Missionary Conference, Edinburgh 1910* (Grand Rapids: Eerdmanns, 2009), 125.
2. World Missionary Conference, *Report of Commission I-VIII: History and Records of the Conference Together with Addresses Delivered at the Evening Meetings*, (Edinburgh and London: Oliphant, Anderson & Ferrier; and New York, Chicago and Toronto: Fleming H. Revell Co., n.d. [1910]), 306–315.
3. Justin Long, ed. and Justin Mandryk, "State of the Gospel," *Momentum*, November/December 2006, http://www.strategicnetwork.org/wp-content/uploads/2008/05/200611.pdf.
4. See Philip Jenkins, *The Next Christendom* (New York: Oxford University Press, rev. ed. 2007), for a comprehensive discussion of these dynamics.
5. See Matthew 16:18.

## One: Stewards of Hope

1. Dr. Shane Lopez, *Gallup Student Poll National Report*, 2009, 2., http://www.americaspromise.org/OurWork/~/media/Files/Our%20Work/Gallup%20Student%20Poll/GSP%20National%20Report.ashx.
2. See Romans 15:4.

3. See Hebrews 6:10-11.
4. Philip Schaff, et al, *Nicene and Post-Nicene Fathers: Series II/Volume I/Church History of Eusebius/ Book VII*, http://en.wikisource.org/wiki/Nicene_ and_PostNicene_Fathers:_Series_II/Volume_I/ Church_History_of_Eusebius/Book_VII/Chapter_22.
5. See James 1:27.
6. Kierkegaard introduced this idea in his treatise *Either/ Or: A Fragment of Life*, and developed it further as he progressed in his own faith journey.
7. C. S. Lewis, *Mere Christianity* (New York: Macmillan, 1960), 169–170.

## Two: The Ecclesia—God's Plan A

1. See 1 Corinthians 15:14.
2. See Matthew 28:18-20.
3. See Acts 1:7-8.
4. See Colossians 1:24.
5. See Acts 2:43; 3:12; 4:7, 30, 33; 5:12.
6. See Acts 4:13, 31.
7. See Acts 5:39-41.
8. See Acts 2:42.
9. See Acts 2:45; 4:32-34.
10. See Acts 4:32.
11. See Acts 2:7, 43; 3:10; 5:11.
12. See Acts 2:41, 47; 4:4: 6:1, 7.
13. As in Acts 7:38, Hebrews 2:12; 12:23.
14. As in Colossians 1:18, 24; Ephesians 1:22.
15. See Ephesians 5:22-32.
16. As in 1 Corinthians 1:2; 1 Thessalonians 1:1. The only exception for this appears in Acts 9:31, where the singular *ecclesia* refers to several geographical locations.

# Notes

17. See Mark 3:7-35.
18. See John 20:19.
19. See Galatians 5:6.
20. *Confessia Augustana*, Article VII opens, "The church is the congregation of saints, in which the Gospel is rightly taught and the Sacraments are rightly administered." http://www.fullbooks.com/The-Augsburg-Confessionx5984.html.
21. Lausanne Committee for World Evangelization, 2004. The local church in mission. www.lausanne.org/documents/2004forum/LOP39_IG10.pdf.
22. Jim Engel and William Dyrness, *Changing the Mind of Missions* (Downers Grove: InterVarsity Press, 2000), 117.
23. See Matthew 20:25-28; Matthew 23:10-12.
24. Howard Synder, *The Community of the King* (Downers Grove: InterVarsity Press, 2004), 77.
25. See Ephesians 2:21-22; 1 Peter 2:5.
26. John Westerhoff III, *Living the Faith Community* (Minneapolis: Winston Press, 1985), 69.

## Three: The One Thing—Disciple-Making

1. Rob Bell and Don Golden, *Jesus Wants to Save Christians* (Grand Rapids: Zondervan, 2008).
2. Greg Hawkins and Cally Parkinson, *Reveal: Where Are You?* (South Barrington, IL: Willow Creek Association, 2007).
3. George Barna, *Growing True Disciples* (Colorado Springs: Waterbrook, 2001).
4. See 2 Peter 3:12.
5. See 1 Corinthians 15:13-18.
6. The noun *disciple* (*mathetes*) is common in the Gospels and Acts, but did not appear in the rest of the New

Testament. It appears 73 times in Matthew, 46 in Mark, and 37 in Luke. Mark and Luke used the noun to describe the twelve, while Matthew used the word more widely; it included the twelve, but not exclusively.
7. Bill Hull, *Christlike* (Colorado Springs: NavPress, 2010), 14.
8. See James 1:22.
9. See Acts 4:34.
10. Chris Sugden, *Radical Discipleship* (London: Marshall, Morgan & Scott, 1981), 128.
11. Dallas Willard, *Renovation of the Heart* (Colorado Springs: NavPress, 2002).
12. Dallas Willard, *The Divine Conspiracy* (New York: Harper Collins, 1998), 281.
13. Ibid., 271.
14. See John 10:9-10.

## Four: Children as Disciples

1. Willard, *The Divine Conspiracy*, 272.
2. Dan Brewster, "The 4/14 Window: Child Ministries and Mission Strategy in Children," in *Children in Crisis: A New Commitment.* Phyllis Kilbourn, ed. (Pasadena: MARC Publications, 1996).
3. Bryant Myers, "The State of the World's Children: A Cultural Challenge to the Christian Mission in the 1990s." Presented at the Evangelical Fellowship of Mission Agencies executive retreat, Colorado Springs, CO, September 1992.
4. George Barna, *Transforming Children into Spiritual Champions* (Ventura: Regal, 2003), 34
5. Hawkins and Parkinson, *Reveal: Where Are You?*
6. Dan Brewster, *Future Impact* (Colorado Springs: Compassion International, 2010).

# Notes

7. See Luke 1:41.
8. Willard, *The Divine Conspiracy*, 291.
9. See Luke 5:11.
10. See Matthew 20:32-34.
11. UNICEF, "Child Survival and Health," http://www.child-info.org/mortality.html (accessed November 10, 2009).
12. Cited by Norman Herr, "Television and Health," *Internet Resources to Accompany the Sourcebook for Teaching Science*, http://www.csun.edu/science/health/docs tv&health.html#tv_stats.

## Five: Global Connections, Local Relationships

1. See Acts 11:23.
2. See Acts 11:28-30.
3. See Ephesians 4:16.
4. The three authors of this book are part of Compassion International, an organization dedicated to partnering with the Ecclesia in its mandate of making disciples, focusing specifically on the discipling of children living in poverty.
5. See John 17:20-23.
6. *History and Records of the Conference* (see Introduction, n. 2), 306-315.